Flip it

Gymnastics

SPORTS STARTERS

Paul Challen

 Crabtree Publishing Company

www.crabtreebooks.com

SPORTS STARTERS

Created by Bobbie Kalman

Author
Paul Challen

Project coordinator
Kathy Middleton

Editors
Janine Belzak
Molly Aloian
Rachel Stuckey

Photo research
Melissa McClellan

Design
Tibor Choleva
Melissa McClellan

Production coordinator
Ken Wright

Prepress technician
Ken Wright

Photographs
Helen Cooper, photographersdirect.com: pages 6, 7, 10, 11, 13, 14, 15, 20, 21, 25
John Cheng: pages 12, 18, 19, 29
Ilan Rosen, photographersdirect.com: page 23
Shutterstock.com: cover; pages 1, 5, 16, 17, 22, 30
iStockphoto.com: back cover; pages 3, 4, 26
bigstockphoto.com: page 27
Bettmann/CORBIS: page 24
Wally McNamee/CORBIS: page 28

Special thanks to
Cristina Bontas-Tantaru, Gabi Tantaru, World Class Gymnastics, Helen Cooper and John Cheng

Created for Crabtree Publishing by Silver Dot Publishing

Library and Archives Canada Cataloguing in Publication

Challen, Paul, 1967-
    Flip it gymnastics / Paul Challen.

(Sports starters)
Includes index.
ISBN 978-0-7787-3144-3 (bound).--ISBN 978-0-7787-3176-4 (pbk.)

    1. Gymnastics--Juvenile literature. I. Title. II. Series: Sports starters (St. Catharines, Ont.)

GV461.3.C43 2010   j796.44   C2009-906937-7

Library of Congress Cataloging-in-Publication Data

Challen, Paul C. (Paul Clarence), 1967-
Flip it gymnastics / Paul Challen.
    p. cm. -- (Sports starters)
Includes index.
ISBN 978-0-7787-3176-4 (pbk. : alk. paper) -- ISBN 978-0-7787-3144-3 (reinforced library binding : alk. paper)
1. Gymnastics--Juvenile literature. I. Title. II. Series.

GV461.3.C53 2010
796.44--dc22
                                                            2009048049

Crabtree Publishing Company

www.crabtreebooks.com   1-800-387-7650

Printed in the U.S.A./122009/CG20091120

Published in Canada
Crabtree Publishing
616 Welland Ave.
St. Catharines, Ontario
L2M 5V6

Published in the United States
Crabtree Publishing
PMB 59051
350 Fifth Avenue, 59th Floor
New York, New York 10118

Published in the United Kingdom
Crabtree Publishing
Maritime House
Basin Road North, Hove
BN41 1WR

Published in Australia
Crabtree Publishing
386 Mt. Alexander Rd.
Ascot Vale (Melbourne)
VIC 3032

Contents

What is gymnastics?

Gymnastics is an indoor sport that is made up of many different **exercises**. People who do gymnastics are called **gymnasts**. Gymnasts need to be strong and flexible to do these exercises. Some gymnastics exercises are simple. Others are complicated. With a little bit of practice, it is easy to perform simple gymnastics moves. But the complicated moves take many hours of practice to perform.

Gymnastics takes a lot of concentration.

Floor exercises require flexibility and agility.

Something for everyone

Gymnasts perform on all kinds of equipment. Girls perform on four **events**: **vault**, uneven **bars**, **balance beam**, and floor. Boys perform on six events: floor, vault, **pommel horse**, **rings**, parallel bars, and high bar.

Fun and fitness

Practicing gymnastics is a great way to build up your strength. You need power in your arms and legs to do **tumbling** moves and jumps. As well, your muscles need to stretch easily to do many gymnastics skills. It is also important to be **agile** in gymnastics, so you can move around with grace. Gymnasts need good balance to perform moves properly.

Practicing gymnastics on a team is a great way to make friends and have fun.

Judges look for strengths and weaknesses in a routine, as well as how difficult it is.

The competitive side

Gymnastics can also be a competitive sport. In a gymnastics competition, gymnasts put their moves together in a **routine**. People called **judges**, watch the routine carefully. Judges give each routine a number, called the **score**. The fewer mistakes a gymnast makes in his or her routine, the higher the score.

A lot going on!

During a gymnastics competition, there is always a lot of action. Some athletes are performing on the floor. Others are practicing moves on the rings. Over on the parallel bars, the uneven bars, and the high bar, gymnasts perform swing movements. On the pommel horse and balance beam, gymnasts test their strength and balance. Gymnasts on vault run fast and launch themselves into the air.

The judges' angle

Gymnasts sometimes gather for a competition. During a competition, **coaches** help the gymnasts warm up and prepare their routines. Judges are also there, giving out scores to the gymnasts for their routines.

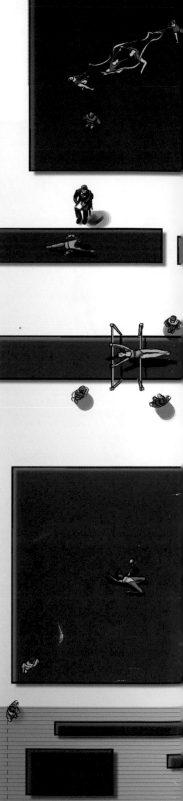

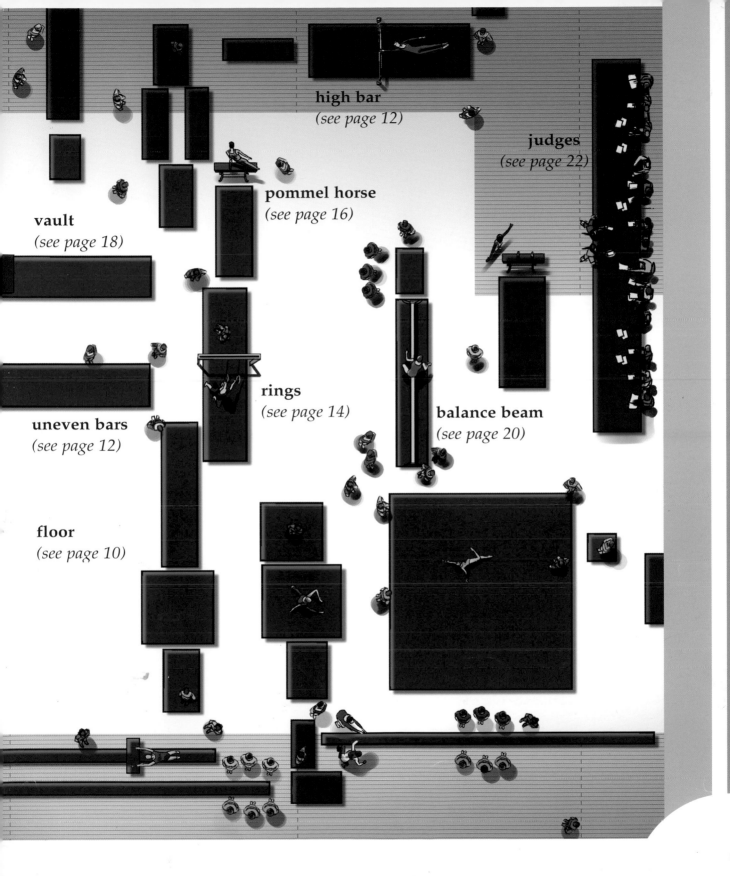

high bar
(see page 12)

judges
(see page 22)

pommel horse
(see page 16)

vault
(see page 18)

rings
(see page 14)

balance beam
(see page 20)

uneven bars
(see page 12)

floor
(see page 10)

On the floor

Floor exercises include some of the most exciting moves in gymnastics. Both boys and girls perform on the floor. A gymnast does not need any special equipment on the floor. He or she does tumbling moves—like somersaults—that test agility. The floor is the place to test a gymnast's strength with moves like **handstands**, **handsprings**, and **saltos**, or flips. Female gymnasts perform their routines to music.

Strength and power are important in tumbling.

Good form and graceful movements make a good floor routine.

Spring time

Gymnasts perform their floor routines on a special **mat**. It is called a **spring floor** because it has springs or foam under it to give gymnasts extra bounce when they perform their skills.

Bar none!

The bar events test a gymnast's strength and flexibility. Girls perform on the uneven bars. Boys perform on the parallel bars and high bar. On the bar events, gymnasts perform swinging movements, handstands, and release moves in which the gymnast briefly lets go of the bar. Once a gymnast has finished the routine, he or she flies off the bars and lands on the floor. This move is called a **dismount**.

On the uneven bars, athletes must perform skills on both the low and high bars.

Up and down

The uneven bars are two bars that are set at different heights above the ground. The parallel bars are both set at the same height above the ground, next to each other. The high bar is a single bar, set high above the ground so that when a gymnast swings on it, his feet do not touch the ground.

Exercises on the parallel bars require a lot of arm strength.

Ring it up

The rings event requires strength and control. Only boys perform on the rings. The rings look very simple. They are just two rings hanging from a metal frame, high above the ground. A gymnast grabs the rings and holds all of his weight above the ground with his arms and hands. The exercises a gymnast does on the rings are a test of strength and balance.

CONTINENTAL

milano

Gymnasts must keep the rings as still as possible while performing skills.

Mastering the iron cross means developing powerful shoulders and arms.

Not for beginners!

It takes a long time for a gymnast to perform a move called an **iron cross**. To do an iron cross, the gymnast grabs the rings and pulls himself up by spreading his arms wide. The gymnast's body is in the shape of a cross. Imagine the strength it takes to do this exercise!

Horsing around

Only boys perform on the pommel horse. The gymnast grabs onto pommels, or handles. He supports his weight on his hands while performing swinging movements with his legs. A gymnast must travel from one end of the horse to the other without brushing it with his legs. When the gymnast is finished his routine, he uses his arms to push off the horse into the dismount.

Gymnasts must swing above the pommel horse handles.

Not a real horse

The pommel horse has a metal frame. The frame is covered in leather, and the horse's handles have special grips. The horse was invented in ancient times to give soldiers a way to practice getting on and off a real horse.

To perform a scissors move, a gymnast swings one leg and then the other above the horse.

Vaulting for glory

Vaulting is all about speed, power, and control! Both boys and girls perform on the vault. Gymnasts start at one end of a long narrow strip called a **runway**. At the other end of the runway is the vaulting table. Just in front of the vaulting table is a springy platform called a **springboard**. Only the gymnast's hands are allowed to touch the vaulting table during a vault.

Without good balance, it is impossible to do difficult moves off the vault.

A need for speed

Gymnasts sprint at top speed down the runway. When they get to the springboard, they bounce hard on it, and put their hands on the vault. Then they fly into the air. When they are in the air, gymnasts perform twists or flips. The gymnast must also perform a solid landing on two feet without stumbling or falling down.

A gymnast completes her vault with a good landing.

Beam me up!

Gymnasts need balance to do all gymnastics events well. But on the balance beam, balance is the most important thing! Only girls perform on the balance beam. On this event, the gymnast climbs on top of a beam that is only four inches (10 cm) wide, and performs a routine. She does turns, jumps, and other complicated moves. These moves would be hard to do on the floor, but they are even harder on the balance beam because the gymnast must not fall off!

Concentration before mounting the balance beam is important to a successful routine.

This gymnast is performing a back handspring on the beam.

Get back up again

If a gymnast does fall off the balance beam, the important thing is that she lands without getting hurt. The gymnast must then jump back up and continue the routine. In a gymnastics competition, a gymnast loses points for falling off the beam.

The official scene

In competitive gymnastics, judges are very important. They are the only people who can decide on a gymnast's score. Judges look at how well gymnasts perform their routines. They also look for mistakes in the routine. Mistakes can be slips, stumbles, or falls.

Judges have a front-row view of the action.

*A coach **spots**, or supports, a gymnast when they are learning new skills.*

Hey, coach!

Gymnasts learn about the different events from coaches. Most coaches are also gymnasts themselves, so they know what it takes to do complicated routines, and how to practice the moves. Coaches are also important because they encourage gymnasts to do their best and teach them how to perform moves safely.

Perfect tens!

Gymnasts often talk about the "perfect 10." That is because, for a long time, a score of 10 was the highest score possible in a gymnastics event. No gymnast had ever scored a perfect 10 in the Olympic Games until Nadia Comaneci of Romania did it in the 1976 Olympics in Montreal, Canada. Nadia was only 14 years old when she earned a perfect score!

Romanian star Nadia Comaneci

Updated scoring

The International Gymnastics Federation (IGF) creates the rules that gymnasts must follow. In 2006, the IGF started a new system of scoring. In this system, gymnasts can score higher than a 10.

Each gymnastics event has its own scoring rules.

Gearing up

Gymnasts do not need a lot of special gear. You can start with comfortable clothing—such as shorts or track pants and a T-shirt—that allows you to move freely. Gymnasts wear stretchy one-piece outfits called **leotards**, as well as other special clothing. Some gymnasts also use **hand grips** for events where it is important to grab on to equipment without slipping.

These girls are wearing hand grips on their hands.

Equipment needed!

To do many of the exercises in gymnastics, gymnasts need some special equipment. Mats, balance beams, and rings are all necessary. So are vaults, pommel horses, and springboards. These pieces of equipment play an important part in the many events that make up gymnastics.

Competition

Gymnastics competitions are held all over the world. Gymnasts of all ages and abilities compete. You do not have to be a superstar to compete in gymnastics. All you need is to practice hard and enjoy the sport!

Every four years, the best gymnasts compete at the Summer Olympics. As well, gymnasts compete in the World Gymnastics Championships every year.

American star Mary Lou Retton

Top stars

Great female gymnasts of the past include Nadia Comaneci, Olga Korbut, and Mary Lou Retton. Some of today's stars are Nastia Liukin of the United States in women's competition, and men's star Chen Yibing of China.

Nastia Liukin of the United States is one of today's top stars.

Flip it up!

Gymnastics is a great sport for fun and fitness. The flexibility and strength a gymnast needs comes in handy in other sports, too. Some school's physical education classes include gymnastics. There are local clubs to join, too. Coaches can help improve a gymnast's moves and teach the gymnast how to perform moves safely.

Teammates can help one another perfect even the toughest routines.

Glossary

Note: Boldfaced words that are defined in the text may not appear in the glossary.

agile Having excellent body control and the ability to move about quickly and gracefully

balance beam A four inch- (10 cm-) wide rail on which female gymnasts perform routines

bars Gymnastics equipment such as the parallel bars, uneven bars, and high bar that a gymnast uses to do complicated exercises

coach A person who supports a gymnast through teaching, practice, and encouragement

events Gymnastics activities involving certain pieces of equipment or styles of movement

exercises Gymnastics activities

floor exercises A series of flips, tumbles, and acrobatic moves done on a gymnastics floor

hand grips Leather hand coverings used by gymnasts in events requiring a good grip

handspring A move in which a gymnast balances upside-down supported by the hands

handstand A move in which a gymnast moves from a standing position to a handstand and back again

mat The surface used underneath gymnastics equipment or for floor routines

pommel horse A gymnastics event in which a gymnast swings his legs over a piece of equipment

rings A gymnastics event using rings to perform skills requiring strength and control

routine A combination of gymnastics moves, sometimes set to music

saltos Acrobatic flips

tumbling Acrobatic moves performed in a row

vault A gymnastics event in which gymnasts use springboards to leap over other equipment

Index